LET'S GET COOKING

LET'S GET COOKING

REBUILDING MACON

REBUILDING MACON | MACON, GEORGIA | 2010

©2010 Rebuilding Macon
3864 Lake Street
Macon, Georgia 31204

LET'S GET COOKING
First Edition

ISBN-10 0-9753726-0-2
ISBN-13 978-0-9753726-0-9

Photography ©2010 Beau Cabell
Book design by Burt&Burt

Printed in Canada

ACKNOWLEDGMENTS

Like the front yard of Mr. Baker's house on Rebuilding Day—crowded with many volunteers, ready to fire it up—the effort of many hands helped to hammer out *Let's Get Cooking*.

We are grateful to our Board of Directors for allowing us to pursue this project and support us along the way.

We are also very grateful to the owners and chefs of each restaurant represented in this cookbook for their willingness to share a little bit of their history and their recipes with us.

A very special thank you to James and Jodi Palmer for seeing this project as we saw it, and for sending us down the correct path to complete it.

A big, big, thank you to Beth Wilson and Joni Woolf for their exceptional editing skills.

We'd also like to thank Skippy Davis for creating profiles that will have you running for the table of one of these restaurants (the nearest one), Beau Cabell, whose photographs will have you drooling, and Jim and Mary-Frances Burt of Burt&Burt Studio for designing the cookbook we've dreamed of.

Last, but not least, we'd like to thank our countless volunteers who work with us to provide rehabilitation services, free of charge, to elderly and disabled low-income homeowners.

We thank each of you for helping us rebuild Macon, one house at a time.

TRUE GRIS

I AM NOT MUCH OF A CARPENTER. I can't plum bob or cut in a straight line. I am sheet-rock challenged. I never seem to have the right kind of screwdriver or remember where I left the hammer.

My wife knows this. That's why when the floor tile needs to be grouted or the door planed, she summons our good friend, Jesse. He is a genius. My wife calls him so often he is on her speed dial.

I'm not much of a cook, either, although I do scramble a mean egg and pretend to watch a lot of cooking shows on The Food Network. I make the coffee every morning and know where most of the buttons are on the microwave.

Actually, I am pretty darn good on the grill. I bought a Big Green Egg a few years ago, and it's one of the best investments I ever made. Love it.

And my "True Gris Stew" is to die for. That's why I've included the recipe as part of the *Let's Get Cooking* cookbook for Rebuilding Macon.

So why am I writing the foreword to this mouth-watering collection of recipes from some of Macon's finest eating establishments?

Well, I've got a few nouns in my toolbox, and keep some verbs and adjectives in my pantry. Maybe they thought I might be able to construct a sentence or two. I will try not to disappoint.

They also probably heard about my legendary kitchen feat of a few years ago when I managed to combine both cooking and power tools.

I am not making this up.

Once upon a time, we had a feature at *The Telegraph* called "From Our Kitchens." Employees either volunteered (or were recruited) to select a recipe from the previous week's food section, whip it up and write about the life-changing experience.

This usually led to plenty of adventures and more than a few misadventures. For my first attempt at this, I picked a recipe for strawberry cake submitted by a Macon man named Ed.

I did not choose the recipe because it looked easy or because I was particularly fond of strawberries. It was selected because the man's name was Ed. I have never met another Ed who wasn't a pretty good fellow, so I believed this to be a safe choice.

I made it through the cake part without any incidents. (Thank you, Betty Crocker.) It was the icing that prompted the restraining order from all future dessert recipes.

When I gathered the ingredients together and was ready to stir, I could only find the blades to the electric mixer. My wife confessed her mother had borrowed it. My in-laws lived across town and it was already way past dark.

I had to quickly put on my thinking cap, which comes in adjustable sizes. I went to my tool box and found my Black & Decker drill. The blades fit perfectly! I patted myself on the back as I returned to the kitchen.

However, I failed to account for the fact that power drills have only one speed—very high. So a large portion of the extremely colorful strawberry icing ended up in my hair and on the kitchen walls.

At least the cake was delicious and received fabulous reviews from the vultures in the newsroom. I had my photograph taken with the drill and made my debut in the Wednesday food section.

By that afternoon, I had received an endorsement from Black & Decker to use its new band saw to slice tomatoes. (OK, I made that part up.)

So, yes, I have achieved a mixed marriage of culinary skills and home demolition.

My only other food-related notoriety is having the Monte Cristo sandwich at Molly's Café named after me. Owner Betty Mock honored me by renaming the popular menu item the "Monte Gristo." It's yummy.

Many thanks to all the folks at Rebuilding Macon and the dedicated volunteers who do so much to make our city a better place to live and to bring a measure of pride back to so many homeowners.

Bon appetit, y'all.

Ed Grisamore is a columnist for The (Macon) Telegraph. *He is the author of six books and winner of the 2010 Will Rogers Humanitarian Award, presented by the National Society of Newspaper Columnists.*

TRUE GRIS STEW

INGREDIENTS

1 pound ground beef, browned and drained
1 pound BBQ
3 boneless chicken breasts
4 cans sliced tomatoes
4 cans sliced potatoes
4 cans whole grain corn
1 can cream corn
1 can tomato sauce
2 cans english peas
1 can beef broth
1 bottle ketchup (to taste)
1/4 cup Tabasco sauce

PREPARATION

Mix together in large pot. Simmer well.

Makes 20 cups or 10 pints

NOW,

LET'S GET COOKING

13
DOLCE VITA PIZZERIA & CAFE

Georgia Peach Cheesecake

17
DOWNTOWN GRILL

Portabella Rockefeller | Jamaican Jerk Chicken | White Chocolate Macadamia Nut Cookie

23
GRITS CAFE

Fried Green Tomatoes | Praline Chicken Breast | White Chocolate Banana Cream Pie

28
JENEANE'S

Flat Bread | Turnip Greens | Rutabagas | Cornbread Dressing | Chocolate Pie

35
KUDZU CATERING

Andouille Stuffed Creole Pork Chops | Lee's Beer Chili
Crab Stuffed Mushrooms | Zipper Pea Hummus

45
LUIGI'S BISTRO

Penne alla Siciliana | Sonny's Cavatappi Stracciatella | Gamberi con Prosciutto

51
MARCO RISTORANTE ITALIANO

Risotto | Lobster Salad | Potatoes Gnocchi

Walter DiZio (left)) with Cesare Mammarella

DOLCE VITA PIZZERIA & CAFE
DEEP DISH PIZZA

LIKE ME, MY COUSIN WALTER DIZIO is from Pescara, Italy, which is in the Abruzzo region. His experience there in the restaurant business is extensive, including ownership of both a fine dining restaurant and a brick oven pizzeria. His menus were developed and representative of the local farmers, butchers, bakers and dairymen.

I asked my cousin to come to Macon and help develop a pizza dough for Dolce Vita Pizzeria & Cafe. The challenges were many. You must understand, deep-dish pizza was born in Chicago, not Italy. Italian pizza is thin and cooked in brick ovens at temperatures exceeding 700 degrees. Also, the natural composition of the three vital components of pizza—water, climate and flour—are completely different here from those in Italy.

Deep-dish pizza was born in Chicago during World War II. In a regular pizza the sauce goes on first and the cheese last. With deep-dish pizza it is the opposite. Regular pizza slides into an oven on a paddle, whereas a deep-dish pizza is cooked in a pan two inches deep. While visiting Chicago I fell in love with this unique pizza and since then have wanted to reproduce it here in Macon.

Dolce Vita soon became engulfed in an atmosphere of experimentation. After a month of testing, our dough recipe was born. Next, Walter used his experience to develop the quality recipes for the filling. Our sauce is seasoned the way it would be in Italy. Our cheeses are top grade, not oil-based cheese substitutes so common in many pizzas. Most pizzerias put the mushrooms on raw, with no seasoning. Before our mushrooms go into a pizza, they are seasoned with fresh chopped garlic, Mediterranean salt, extra-virgin olive oil and fresh chopped parsley, and then oven-baked. Our Macon deep-dish pizza, unlike Chicago's, has an extra layer of cheese. We complete the last five minutes of bake time with another layer of cheese prior to serving, bringing out the flavor of the baked cheese perfectly.

You see, Walter's inexperience with typical American pizza, whether deep-dish or not is what truly makes this Macon version of deep-dish pizza unique and delicious. His experience with the rustic simplicity and layered flavors of his pizza in Italy completes our deep-dish pizza journey here in the States. Our deep-dish pizza has since developed a cult-like following in Macon.

The beauty of all this for me is not only the pleasure of working with my cousin but also that there is only one place in the world one can get such a pizza: Macon, Georgia.

Cesare Mammarella

GEORGIA PEACH CHEESECAKE

INGREDIENTS

CRUST

1 cup graham cracker crumbs

2 tablespoons sugar

3 tablespoons melted butter

CAKE

6-8 ounces cream cheese, softened

2 tablespoons flour

1 teaspoon vanilla

1 cup sugar

3/4 cup sour cream

5 eggs

4 Georgia peaches,
peeled and sliced

PREPARATION

Preheat oven to 300 degrees.

CRUST Mix crust ingredients and press onto bottom of 9-inch spring form pan. Bake 10 minutes.

CAKE Beat cream cheese, flour, vanilla, and sugar on medium speed until well blended. Add sour cream and mix.

Add eggs one at a time and beat on low speed until blended. Add 2 chopped peaches into mixture. Pour mixture over crust.

Bake 1 hour or until the center is set. Refrigerate for 5 hours and top with the other 2 peaches.

Richie Jone

DOWNTOWN GRILL

WORD OF MOUTH has made the Downtown Grill a favorite spot for local diners and tourists who are looking for white tablecloth dining in an upscale, casual atmosphere. "We see a combination of familiar faces and out-of-town visitors who hear about us through the hotels, the Convention and Visitors Bureau and local promotions," said owner Richie Jones.

Jones, a graduate of First Presbyterian Day School and the University of Georgia, says his early entry into the restaurant business came when he "got a job in a restaurant hoping to learn to cook." Since then, he managed Spanky's in Brunswick for five years and also the Sea Island Beach Club before returning to Macon and buying the Downtown Grill in 2008.

The restaurant, which opened in 1997, already had a thriving clientele that has grown. Downtown Grill customers include the over-50 set who have been coming in for years, plus college students and young professionals. "People come here, enjoy themselves, and then come back again," he said.

The blue cheese stuffed filet and the goat cheese and cranberry stuffed filets are by far the most popular items on the menu. "Our desserts get a lot of publicity, too," he added, "whether the White Chocolate Macadamia Nut Cookie with vanilla bean ice cream or the honey amaretto ice cream pie."

A cigar and martini bar adds to the delights customers find at the Downtown Grill. "When you dine with us, you get a great meal in a comfortable atmosphere," Jones said.

PORTABELLA ROCKEFELLER

INGREDIENTS

4 portabella mushrooms
3 garlic cloves
1/4 cup red onions
pinch of salt
1/4 pound bacon
1 ounce olive oil
12 ounces baby spinach
8 ounces mozzarella cheese

Serves 4

PREPARATION

Fry bacon in saute pan and drain grease. Chop the bacon into small pieces. Put aside.

Break stems off mushrooms and use a spoon and scrape out the dark area under the mushroom caps. Finely dice the red onions.

Mince the garlic and saute it in the bacon pan with the olive oil, spinach, onion, and bacon. Toss in a pinch of salt to season it. Cook ingredients until the spinach cooks down.

While this is cooking put the mushrooms on the grill for 2 minutes. When all is cooked put the spinach mix on top of the mushroom caps, then top with the cheese and put it into an oven until the cheese has melted.

Cut into triangular slices.

JAMAICAN JERK CHICKEN
OVER ROMAINE LETTUCE
WITH A PINEAPPLE-GINGER DRESSING

INGREDIENTS

PINEAPPLE-GINGER DRESSING

1 small can pineapple juice

1/4 cup soy sauce

1/4 cup salad oil

1/4 cup extra virgin olive oil

2 teaspoons honey

2 teaspoons finely grated ginger

4 cloves garlic, minced

large pinch of crushed
red pepper flakes

1 1/4 cup small diced
fresh pineapple

1 tablespoon fresh lime juice

1 tablespoon Sesame seeds

JAMAICAN JERK CHICKEN

Jamaican Jerk seasoning from store

4, 9-ounce chicken breasts

2 heads romaine lettuce

16 cherry tomatoes

Pineapple-Ginger Dressing

PREPARATION

First make the dressing by combining all ingredients.

Next, rinse and cut the heads of romaine and portion them into
4 equal size salads.

Pour the dressing over top and mix it well and top each of these with
4 cherry tomatoes.

Cook the chicken breast on a hot skillet with a little butter and the jerk
seasoning.

When the chicken is cooked, cut it into thin strips and top the salad
with it.

Pair with a nice, crisp Sauvignon Blanc.

Serves 4

WHITE CHOCOLATE MACADAMIA NUT COOKIE

INGREDIENTS

1 1/2 cups sifted flour

1 teaspoon baking powder

1/8 teaspoon salt

1 egg

1 cup brown sugar

1 1/2 teaspoon pure vanilla extract

1 cup melted butter

4 ounces white chocolate

1/2 cup Macadamia nuts

1 pint Breyer's Vanilla Bean ice cream

chocolate syrup

PREPARATION

Preheat oven to 325 degrees.

Mix the first three ingredients: flour, baking powder, and salt.

Next, combine the remaining ingredients (except the ice cream) and add to flour mixture. Mix well.

Form into 2-ounce patties. Place them on a tray at room temperature for 30 minutes.

Cook at 325 degrees for 10 minutes.

When the cookies have cooled, make a 1-inch thick disc of ice cream and put it between 2 cookies.

Place in a freezer and let it mold together, then serve frozen topped with chocolate syrup.

Serves 4

Wayne Wetendorf

GRITS CAFE

SOUTHERN HOSPITALITY and a creative approach to true Southern-style food keep customers coming back to the Grits Cafe. Since opening in 1999 on the downtown square in Forsyth, Georgia, owners Terri and Wayne Wetendorf have created an alluring menu and a charming atmosphere of fine and friendly service.

Chef Wayne blends Southern traditional cooking with touches of what's new and trendy. "I like to keep the menu interesting," he said, "and we use many local products." Buying from area farmers' markets and local growers ensures that the ingredients are the freshest available.

"We are following the trend toward green and organic, and as small business owners we like to support other small businesses, too," Terri said.

Grits Cafe has become a popular spot for birthday and anniversary celebrations and is a neighborhood favorite for locals.

"We spend a lot of time coaching our staff on the art of delivering exceptional hospitality," Terri said. "We try hard to provide proper service, paying attention to the details, but never pretentious. Making our guests feel at home is very important."

The menu is extensive, and boutique wines are available to complement the excellent fare. There's also a full bar and a martini menu to suit every taste.

Grits Cafe's diners come from all around. "We're in several travel books and that has brought us the 'snowbirds' who travel through twice a year," said Terri. "We've gotten to know many of them who plan their trips based around an overnight stop in Forsyth to dine at Grits Cafe. "We never imagined when we opened that we would build such a big, loyal following."

FRIED GREEN TOMATOES

INGREDIENTS

TOMATOES

peanut oil

4 medium green tomatoes,
sliced a quarter-inch thick

2 cups seasoned flour

3 eggs, whisked

3 cups white bread crumbs

REMOULADE

1/4 cup mayonnaise

1/4 cup sour cream

1 small onion, finely diced

2 sticks of celery, finely diced

1 dill pickle, finely diced

1 jalapeño pepper, finely diced

1/3 cup marinara sauce

ASSEMBLY

1/2 pound cooked shrimp

chopped chives, parsley
(for garnish)

PREPARATION

TOMATOES Preheat oil to 325 degrees in a frying pan.

In three separate shallow dishes, put flour, egg wash, and bread crumbs. Dredge tomatoes in flour, then egg, and finally bread crumbs, coating tomatoes completely. Fry in oil 2-3 minutes.

REMOULADE Combine all ingredients. Season to taste.

ASSEMBLY Place a fried tomato on serving plate, top with remoulade and then an even layer of shrimp. Continue to stack tomatos, shrimp and sauce until there are four layers.

Garnish with chopped chive or parsley and serve.

Serves 1

PRALINE CHICKEN BREAST

INGREDIENTS

2 tablespoons butter

4 tablespoons sugar

1 cup pecan halves

1 cup white bread crumbs

1 cup course ground pecans

1/4 cup brown sugar

4, 6-ounce boneless chicken breasts

8 ounces chèvre goat cheese

1 cup fresh spinach leaves

1 cup seasoned flour

1/4 cup melted butter

2 ounces shallots, minced

3 ounces dry red wine

1 cup heavy cream

1 ounce honey

PREPARATION

Preheat oven to 350 degrees.

Over medium heat in a sauté pan, melt butter and sugar together. Add pecan halves and stir together until sugar has melted completely. Pour onto parchment paper. Reserve.

Combine the bread crumbs, ground pecans, and brown sugar. Reserve.

Cut a pocket into the chicken breast starting at the thick end being careful not to cut through the other end of the breast. Fold together the cheese and spinach.

Divide into 4 equal parts and stuff into chicken breasts. Heat the sauté pan to a medium-high heat.

Dredge chicken breast in seasoned flour; add half the melted butter to the pan and then sauté chicken breasts for two minutes on each side. Remove from pan. Add shallots and sauté for 1 minute. Deglaze with red wine and reduce by half. Add cream and reduce by half or to sauce consistency. Add honey. Reserve.

Roll chicken breasts in remaining melted butter and then coat evenly with pecan-crumb mixture around entire breast. Bake for approximately 15 minutes until done.

Divide sauce onto four plates. Arrange candied pecans in and around sauce. Cut chicken breast in half on an angle and display over sauce.

Serves 4

WHITE CHOCOLATE BANANA CREAM PIE

INGREDIENTS

CRUST
4 ounces white chocolate
4 ounces heavy cream
10 ounces graham crumbs

MOUSSE
8 ounces white chocolate
2 ounces butter
3 egg yolks
1 ounce crème de cacao
4 egg whites
3 tablespoons sugar
4 ounces heavy cream

ASSEMBLY
4 bananas
2 tablespoons brown sugar

PREPARATION

CRUST Melt chocolate together and add cream. Stir in graham crumbs. Press into four tart shells and refrigerate.

MOUSSE Melt chocolate, stirring in butter until completely melted. Add yolks one at a time, mixing completely before adding the next. Add crème de cacao. Beat egg whites to soft peaks. Add sugar and beat to stiff peaks. Fold into chocolate mixture. Whip heavy cream into soft peaks. Fold onto chocolate mixture. Refrigerate.

ASSEMBLY Remove the crust from molds and place onto the plates. Divide the mousse evenly onto crusts. Peel and slice bananas into 1/4-inch ovals. Arrange bananas on top of mousse. Sprinkle each pie evenly with brown sugar. Caramelize (melt) sugar with a propane torch. Serve immediately. You can top with berries or strawberry sauce as an alternative.

Serves 4

JENEANE'S

JENEANE BARBER grew up working in her family's kitchen at home where everyone pitched in, including her grandparents. Planning meals and cooking good food were everyday events in her early life. "It just came natural to me," she said. "If you're young and succeed at something, you just love it."

An active, busy person by nature, Jeneane disliked school, preferring to work. At an early age she began waiting tables in local restaurants. She said that her primary experience in cooking for discerning customers came from the two years she served as head chef at Natalia's. That experience, plus her natural talent for knowing what tastes good, led Jeneane to go out on her own. "I can taste something and tell you what's in it, or tell you what it needs," she said.

In 1989, Jeneane opened her own downtown site, which is now operated by her sister Abby Gordon, serving breakfast and lunch. In 1999, she opened Jeneane's at Pinebrook on Forsyth Road, where her tasty lunches and suppers draw between 500 and 700 diners daily.

Keeping that many diners happy day in and day out "is not a 9 to 5 job," Jeneane said. But she loves to serve up what her customers want. "It's just country cooking," she said. "They love our dressing, which is made from scratch with homemade chicken stock. Our Chicken Tenders are popular—I don't brine the chicken—and a favorite dessert is the banana pudding, which is also made from scratch and served warm."

For many people, dining at Jeneane's is a social occasion because they are sure to see many friends whenever they go there. "We're locally owned and operated, and we love our customers," Jeneane said.

Jackie Smith (left) and Jeneane Barber

FLAT BREAD AND
TURNIP GREENS WITH ROOTS

FLAT BREAD INGREDIENTS

2 cups self-rising cornmeal

1 pinch salt

2 pinches sugar

1 egg

1 cup buttermilk

1 cup milk

1 1/2 cups water

corn or canola oil (may use light oil)

FLAT BREAD PREPARATION

Mix dry ingredients. Mix egg, buttermilk, milk, and water. Mix both dry and wet ingredients together and let set for 10 minutes to rise. If mixture becomes too thick, add a little more water. Add a small amount of oil to frying pan or electric skillet when hot, though not smoking. Drop spoonfuls of mixture in small amounts onto frying pan or skillet. Cook 2 minutes then flip and cook other side.

Serves 6

TURNIP INGREDIENTS

1 gallon water

ham bone, ham pieces or fresh neck bones

1 bunch turnips with roots

3 tablespoons salt

2 tablespoons sugar

1/2 tablespoon cayenne pepper or to taste

1 bunch mustard greens

TURNIP PREPARATION

In a large pot add water and cooking meat of choice. Bring to a boil and reduce to simmer for 45 minutes.

Wash turnips and roots. Cut up turnips into 1-inch to 2-inch strips, removing any large veins. Peel and dice roots into small half-inch pieces.

After cooking meat for 45 minutes remove from pot.

Add other seasonings to pot, then add greens and cook 45 minutes on low heat. Then you will need to add turnip roots and let cook for another 15 minutes.

Serves 8

RUTABAGAS AND CORNBREAD DRESSING

RUTABAGA INGREDIENTS

2-3 large rutabagas
1 gallon water
2 tablespoons black pepper
1 tablespoon salt
2 tablespoons sugar
1/2 stick butter or margarine

RUTABAGA PREPARATION

Peel off waxed skin of rutabagas and cut up into slices. In medium pot add water and other seasonings and bring to boil. Add rutabagas. Reduce heat and simmer on low for about 30 minutes with lid on until rutabagas are tender. Drain off some of the water and add butter or margarine. You may need to add more seasoning according to taste.

Serves 8

DRESSING INGREDIENTS

1/2 gallon turkey or chicken broth (fresh when possible)
9 biscuits, cooked
1 pan cooked cornbread
1/2 onion, crushed in blender
2 celery stalks, crushed in blender
1/2 cup milk
2 eggs
1 tablespoon salt
1 tablespoon pepper
1 tablespoon poultry seasoning

DRESSING PREPARATION

Preheat oven to 400 degrees.

Bring broth to boil in a pot. In a large bowl put the biscuits and cornbread crumbled up; add onion and celery. Pour broth on top and stir; let cool. Add milk, eggs, salt, pepper, and poultry seasoning and stir well. The mixture should be very soupy. Taste to see if you need to add more salt and pepper for your liking. Pour into a baking pan and cook at 400 degrees for 30-45 minutes until brown on top.

Serves 8

CHOCOLATE PIE

INGREDIENTS

2 pre-cooked pie crust shells

4 cups milk

2 cups sugar

$^1/_2$ teaspoon cream of tartar

6 eggs

6 tablespoons corn starch

6 tablespoons cocoa

PREPARATION

Separate eggs, whites in one bowl and yolks in another bowl. Mix milk, 1 $^1/_2$ cups of sugar, and egg yolk, heating on medium heat until hot. Add corn starch until thick. Remove from heat and stir in cocoa. Set aside.

In mixing bowl, put egg whites, the remaining $^1/_2$ cup of sugar and $^1/_2$ teaspoon of cream of tartar and mix on high speed until whites come to peak.

Pour chocolate mixture into pie crust and then put egg white mixture on top and place under broiler until lightly brown.

Yield: 2 pies

Lee Clack

KUDZU CATERING

KUDZU CATERING has gained a huge following since opening in 2006, serving specialties that can't be found anywhere else. Owners Lee Clack and Kelley Wrigley were delighted, and none of their clients were surprised, when Kudzu Catering won the 2010 Best of the Best Catering award from *The Telegraph*.

Lee grew up in a family that enjoyed working together in the kitchen to create flavorful dishes. "As I got older, I learned more about culinary diversity," Lee said. He was in college, studying horticulture and landscape design, when he began cooking for friends and discovered that he felt more comfortable in the food industry than in the garden.

He worked at T. K. Tripp's in Macon and other restaurants and he also began cooking for friends in what he laughs and calls "the underground years." It soon became apparent that catering was his major talent. "I do diverse menus, and I'm able to create and do whatever people want," he said.

Fried shrimp is his signature dish, and he cooks it and all of his Southern seafood specialties on site. For parties, customers always include his shrimp and grits cakes and his hummus among their hors d'oeuvres.

Most food preparation is done at Kudzu Catering's shop, but the business also offers its popular "intimate dining," in which Clack cooks and serves in the home for two to ten diners. "We do it formally, serving the guests at the dining table, or informally, where they sit and watch the cooking, getting to experience the aromas and learn from me as I work," Clack said.

ANDOUILLE STUFFED CREOLE PORK CHOPS

INGREDIENTS

2 tablespoons olive oil

1/2 pound andouille sausage, diced into 1-inch pieces

1/2 cup yellow onion, diced

1/4 cup red bell pepper, diced

2 tablespoons jalapeño, minced

1/4 cup celery, diced

1 tablespoon minced garlic

4 cups crumbled cornbread

2 cups chicken stock

1 tablespoon salt

1/4 teaspoon cayenne pepper

1/4 cup fresh Italian parsley, chopped

4 bone-in pork loin chops, 8-10 ounces each, marinated overnight *(See marinade recipe.)*

3 tablespoons Chef Paul Prudhomme's Blackened Steak Magic Seasoning

PREPARATION

Prepare Creole Marinade. Pour marinade into a plastic food bag, add pork chops, seal tightly and shake until the meat is well coated. Refrigerate for 3-8 hours.

Preheat oven to 375 degrees.

Add 2 tablespoons olive oil to large sauté pan over medium-high heat. Add andouille sausage to pan and render 3-4 minutes. Add onion, pepper, jalapeño, celery and garlic to pan and continue to sauté for about 5 minutes or until vegetables are slightly translucent. Stir in garlic, cornbread, and chicken stock and mix well. Add salt and cayenne and continue to cook for 3 minutes. Remove from heat and stir in parsley. Set aside and let cool.

Remove chops from marinade and cut a 1-to-2-inch slit in side opposite bone. Stuff each chop with half a cup (or more) of stuffing. Chop will be very full, so tie it with butcher's twine to help keep it closed.

Prepare grill or grill pan. Coat chops lightly with Prudhomme's seasoning. Sear the chops on grill or grill pan for 2-3 minutes on each side then remove to sheet pan and place in preheated oven for 5-7 minutes. Remove chops from pan and allow to cool for 2 minutes and remove twine before serving.

Yeld: 4 Chops

CREOLE MARINADE

1/2 cup white wine

1/2 cup olive oil

1/2 cup cane syrup

1/4 cup creole mustard

1/2 cup yellow onion, chopped

1 tablespoon minced garlic

1/2 teaspoon salt

1/4 teaspoon pepper

1/4 teaspoon cayenne pepper

Place all ingredients in food processor and blend well.

Yield: 2 cups

Tip: Use marinade for shrimp, pork, chicken, or turkey. When grilling, sprinkle meat with Paul Prudhomme's Steak Magic.

37

LEE'S BEER CHILI

INGREDIENTS

2 tablespoons olive oil
1 cup yellow onion, diced
1 large jalapeño, minced
3/4 cup red bell pepper, diced
2 teaspoons garlic, minced
1 pound ground beef
2 teaspoons cayenne pepper
2 teaspoons cumin
4 tablespoons chili powder
1 1/2 teaspoons black pepper
1 1/2 teaspoons salt
1 1/2 teaspoons dried oregano
1 tablespoon sugar
3 vine-ripe tomatoes, large diced pieces
2 cups beer
2, 15-ounce cans large red kidney beans
1 1/4 cups water
1, 6-ounce can tomato paste
3/4 cup fresh cilantro leaves, cut coarsely
2 flour tortillas

PREPARATION

Heat oil in large stock pot then add yellow onion, jalepeño, bell pepper and garlic. Sauté vegetables until slightly translucent.

Add beef to vegetables and continue cooking until beef is browned.

Add spices and sugar and stir, then add tomatoes and continue cooking an additional 5 minutes.

Add beer slowly, scraping bottom of pot. Let beer reduce for 5 minutes.

Add kidney beans, water and tomato paste. Bring back to simmer and add cilantro.

Place flour tortillas in processor bowl and chop with metal blade until the consistency of fine bread crumbs. Add tortilla crumbs to pot. Simmer with partial lid for 20-30 minutes.

Tip: Serve topped with cheddar cheese and cilantro.

Yield: 2 quarts

CRAB STUFFED MUSHROOMS

INGREDIENTS

25 baby portabello mushroom caps

1 teaspoon minced garlic
1 cup monterey jack cheese, shredded
1 teaspoon Texas Pete hot sauce
1/4 cup green onion, chopped
1/2 teaspoon salt

1 pound lump crabmeat,
    picked clean of shell bits
1/2 medium jalapeño, minced
1 teaspoon worcestershire sauce
1/4 cup mayonnaise
1/4 cup parmesan cheese, grated

PREPARATION

Preheat oven to 350 degrees.

Clean mushroom caps with dry paper towel and set aside.

Combine remaining ingredients in large bowl.

Stuff each mushroom cap with crab mixture and place on sheet pan lined with parchment. Bake for approximately 30 minutes or until tops begin to brown slightly.

Remove from oven and let stand 2-3 minutes before serving.

Tip: After removing from oven, move to paper towel to absorb excess liquid

Yield: 25

ZIPPER PEA HUMMUS

INGREDIENTS

1/2 pound frozen zipper peas
(butter peas are an acceptable substitute)

1/2 cup yellow onion, chopped

2 teaspoons minced garlic

1/2 teaspoon salt

1/4 teaspoon black pepper

1/8 teaspoon cayenne pepper

1/4 teaspoon cumin

2 tablespoons lemon juice

1/4 cup olive oil

PREPARATION

Add peas and onions to appropriate sized pot and cover with 2 inches of water. Bring to a boil and simmer for approximately 30 minutes or until peas are soft and onions are translucent.

Remove peas from heat and drain, saving some of the liquid.

Put peas in processor and add 2 tablespoons of reserved liquid, garlic, salt, pepper, cayenne, and cumin. Process until smooth. If too thick, add some of reserved juice.

Slowly add lemon juice and then olive oil into processor while running.

Yield: 2 cups

Luis Quevedo

LUIGI'S BISTRO

LUIGI'S BISTRO OPENED on Macon's Cherry Street in January 2003, offering a large menu and Italian ambience. "For every 10 Mexican restaurants there's only one Italian restaurant," Cesare said. "Hey, I'm Italian, so I thought it would be nice to do something close to my heart in downtown, something cool, with a bistro style."

Luigi's and the Tic Toc Room (*page 89*) are located within sight of each other, so a short walk enables Cesare to pop in and out of each one. He and his staff like to stop at the tables to greet diners, who find a friendly welcome at both restaurants.

Cesare loves to cook, too, and sometimes he invades Luigi's large kitchen to whip up a tasty dish himself with Chef Luis Quevedo. "Chef Luis has truly mastered the infusion of the correct sauce with the correct type of pasta—which is the key to Italian Pasta. Most Italian restaurants here will pair any sauce with any pasta, which in Italy is taboo." Maintaining a level of authenticity is one of the reasons for Luigi's success.

Less formal than Tic Toc—shorts and t-shirts are OK at Luigi's—the restaurant is popular with families and college students. "In fact, most of Luigi's staff are Mercer college students," Cesare said.

Tucked inside Luigi's is a second feature, The Wine Cellar at Luigi's Bistro, that doubles as a retail wine store or as a private party room. At any time, you'll find between 90 and 110 small boutique wines there, and they come in a comfortable price range of $12 to $40 a bottle, with some additional higher-end wines available. "The good thing is I carry a bunch of wines that nobody else in town carries," Cesare said. "The bad thing is I have each one for only a few months because I can't get a lot of it due to the small production of these eclectic vineyards."

Luigi's is a prime downtown destination for lunch and supper, drawing shoppers, students, intown dwellers and office denizens to sample its fare with an Italian flair.

PENNE ALLA SICILIANA

INGREDIENTS

1 ounce portabella mushrooms

1/2 ounce roasted red pepper

1 tablespoon vegetable oil

1 tablespoon unsalted butter

4 ounces chicken

1 pinch Cajun seasoning

2 ounces gorgonzola cheese

4 ounces cream sauce

8 ounces cooked penne pasta

1 tablespoon freshly
grated parmigiano cheese

PREPARATION

Sauté mushrooms and peppers in oil and butter.

Add chicken, Cajun seasoning, and gorgonzola cheese.

Add cream and penne pasta. Cook until cream reduces and thickens.

Just before serving put parmigiano in, toss a few times and plate.

Serves 1

SONNY'S CAVATAPPI STRACCIATELLA

INGREDIENTS

3 ounces Italian sausage

4 ounces pomodoro sauce

8 ounces cooked cavatappi pasta

2 ounces shredded mozzarella

pinch of fresh basil

PREPARATION

Cook sausage in oil until brown for at least 3 minutes, grounding it out. Add pomodoro and let cook for 4 minutes or until it thickens.

Add cavatappi pasta and toss. Add mozzarella cheese and toss.

Plate and sprinkle with basil.

Serves 1

GAMBERI CON PROSCIUTTO

INGREDIENTS

7 shrimp

2 ounces mushrooms

3 ounces alfredo cream sauce

8 ounces cooked fettuccine pasta

1 ounce prosciutto

pinch of salt and pepper

1 tablespoon freshly grated
parmigiano cheese

PREPARATION

Pan sear shrimp one minute on each
side on medium heat.

Add mushrooms and alfredo sauce
and cook for 3 minutes or until it
thickens.

Add prosciutto, salt, pepper, and
parmigiano. Toss and plate.

Serves 1

Dario Le

MARCO
RISTORANTE ITALIANO

AN EXCELLENT RESTAURANT, such as Marco, offers top quality food and service, but much more than that, says Nazario Filipponi, owner of Marco on Forsyth Road. "There must also be ambience and some sort of entertainment," he said. That's one reason a house specialty, Branzino, a luscious Mediterranean sea bass, is tenderly baked to perfection on a bed of rock salt, then brought table-side so that the diner and his party can enjoy seeing the expert filleting before the fish is served.

"Seeing it done provides a form of joyful entertainment, and it creates pleasant conversation," Nazario said. Nazario's friend and business partner is the talented chef Dario Leo. The two met in 1995 in Washington, D.C., and Nazario soon discovered that the young chef's dedication to the highest standards of real traditional Italian cooking matched his own. "Dario went to culinary school in Italy and worked with several famous chefs." Nazario said. "I respected his skills, and I told him I would call him to come take a look at Macon."

Eventually, Dario did come to Macon, from the Italian Embassy in Washington, bringing his wife and their growing family.

The restaurant, which opened in 2004, is named Marco because both men have sons of that name. Marco draws customers from as far away as Atlanta, Albany and Americus, and has many faithful local customers as well. "We say thanks to the community and those involved in the business. We have a lot of loyal customers, a following of people happy with our food and atmosphere."

RISOTTO
WITH SAFFRON, ZUCCHINI, AND CRABMEAT

INGREDIENTS

2 tablespoons extra virgin olive oil

1 ounce white onion, chopped

1 medium zucchini, diced

2 pinches saffron

12 ounces Carnaroli rice

1/2 glass of dry white wine

1 quart of vegetable stock

4 ounces jumbo crabmeat

salt and pepper to taste

2 ounces butter

1 ounce parmesan cheese, grated

1 tablespoon of Italian parsley, chopped

PREPARATION

In a medium pot, sauté the extra virgin olive oil and onion until golden.

Add zucchini and saffron. Sauté for 2 minutes then add the rice and sprinkle it with wine. Stir until dry.

Start adding the boiling stock little by little. From this point, the rice will cook in about 15 minutes.

Five minutes before reaching cooking time, add the crab, salt and pepper. Then add butter, cheese and parsley.

Stir for 2 minutes until smooth. Serve.

Serves 4

LOBSTER SALAD
WITH CANTALOUPE AND ASPARAGUS
WITH ORANGE TRUFFLE DRESSING

INGREDIENTS

2 whole 1/2 to 1 pound
live Maine lobsters

20 medium asparagus, blanched

8 slices cantaloupe

ORANGE TRUFFLE DRESSING

1 teaspoon Dijon mustard

2 oranges

1 lemon

4 tablespoons truffle oil

2 tablespoons honey

8 leaves fresh mint, finely chopped

salt and pepper to taste

PREPARATION

Blanch the lobsters in hot boiling water for about 5 to 7 minutes.

Chill them in iced water. Clean them by removing the pulp inside and cut in large pieces.

Cut the asparagus in small pieces along with the cantaloupe in chunks and add to the lobster in a medium salad bowl.

DRESSING In a separate salad bowl, put the mustard, orange peel grates, orange juice, lemon juice, truffle oil, honey, mint, salt and pepper. Whisk vigorously, add to the salad.

Toss and serve chilled.

Serves 4

POTATOES GNOCCHI
WITH FONTINA CHEESE, PARMA PROSCIUTTO, ARTICHOKES AND FRESH TOMATOES

INGREDIENTS

GNOCCHI

1 pound red potatoes
12 ounces all-purpose flour
1/2 teaspoon salt
2 ounces Parmesan cheese
1 pinch nutmeg
1 egg yolk

SAUCE

1 small chopped shallot
4 tablespoons extra virgin oil
1 small bunch fresh thyme
2 fresh artichokes
1/3 cup dry white wine
2 1/2 large Roma tomatoes, diced
1 1/2 cups heavy cream
4 ounces fontina cheese, diced
1 tablespoon grated
Parmesan cheese
salt and pepper to taste

8 thinly sliced
Parma prosciutto slices

PREPARATION

Rinse the potatoes and cook them in their skins in salted water until tender. Remove the potatoes from the water, peel them while hot, and smash them very fine. Put aside to cool. Do not discard the water; you need it to cook the gnocchi later.

Meanwhile, prepare the sauce. In a large skillet, sauté the shallot with extra virgin olive oil and thyme. Once golden in color, add the artichokes (previously cleaned from the hard leaves) cut into julienne strips, and the white wine right after. Once the wine has evaporated, add the fresh tomatoes and cream and let cook for about 5-7 minutes. Then add the fontina and Parmesan cheeses. Let the cheeses melt a little.

Combine the potatoes with the flour and the rest of the ingredients. Knead with the palm of your hand until the dough is smooth and all of the ingredients are incorporated. Remember the dough must be firm, not too soft. Then roll it into a large bread stick shape and cut into half-inch bites.

Cook them in boiling water and once they start floating to the surface, strain them and put them into the sauce. Let the gnocchi simmer for a few minutes. Serve and top with prosciutto.

Serves 4

Betty Mock

MOLLY'S

BETTY MOCK, owner of Molly's on Cherry Street, says she followed a downtown Macon theme in naming her restaurant Molly's. "Even though there's no real Molly, we have Molly's Trolley and Little Richard's "Good Golly, Miss Molly," Betty said, "so the name Molly just seemed right to me. We get a lot of tourists downtown, and they like the name, and they love our Southern hospitality."

Betty and her staff want their customers to feel as comfortable in the restaurant as if they were at home. "So we give them Southern hospitality with a smile, a gracious touch, and show them we're friendly," Betty said. "Since Molly's is like my home, my customers are like my guests. I want them to feel like they're walking into my home."

With embroidered white tablecloths, antiques everywhere, arrangements of Southern flowers, and a vintage look throughout, Molly's is a glimpse of the South as it once was, when ladies wore hats and gloves to town and tea rooms were treasured for their dainty dishes.

But while Molly has the look and feel of a tea room, businessmen have learned they'll find a hearty lunch there. Molly's chef and staff keep them coming back for good Southern cooking.

"It's comfort food," Betty said. "I call it Classic Southern—something a little bit different from everyone else."

Every day brings a special with meat, two vegetables and either cherry cobbler or shortcake for dessert. Ladies love the chicken salad, all white meat served on a croissant with dried cherries, pecans and more. Molly's quiche "is a ladies' thing, but I've gotten the men loving it," Betty said. "In fact, men and women from all over the city head to Cherry Street at lunch for a classic Southern meal. They're never disappointed at Molly's."

MR. ADAM'S
FAVORITE CHICKEN SALAD

INGREDIENTS

3 fresh chicken breasts
1/2 cup chopped celery
1/2 cup pickle relish
1/2 cup pecans
3/4 cup dried cranberries
1/2 cup mayonnaise (Duke's)
1 cup Vidalia onion dressing
1 tablespoon pesto

PREPARATION

Cook chicken until done. Drain stock (save stock for soup).
Let chicken cool, then shred with hands.

Add chopped celery, relish, chopped pecans, dried cranberries, pesto, and mayonnaise.

We add our own Vidalia onion dressing until the salad is moist.
Chill to serve.

Serves 6

MOLLY'S OWN APPLE SALAD

INGREDIENTS

1 quart heavy whipping cream
1 cup sugar
6 Golden Delicious or Granny Smith apples
1/2 cup pecans, chopped
15-ounce can mandarin oranges, drained
1/2 cup crushed pineapple, drained
1/2 bag mini-marshmallows

PREPARATION

In large mixing bowl, mix heavy whipping cream and sugar. Mix with mixer until stiff, then set aside.

Chop apples in small bite-size pieces (you may leave peel on apples) and place in large bowl. Add pecans, mandarin oranges, and pineapples. Mix well. Add whipping cream and marshmallows.

Refrigerate approximately 30 minutes before serving.

Tip: This can be made a day before. Just make sure to soak the apples in lemon.

Serves 12

FRESH SPINACH QUICHE

INGREDIENTS

1, 9-inch deep-dish pie shell

3 eggs

1 cup shredded sharp cheese
(or any cheese desired)

1 cup milk or heavy cream

1 handful fresh spinach (chopped)

seasoning to taste

PREPARATION

Preheat oven to 350 degrees.

Put pie shell in oven until slightly brown.

Mix eggs, cheese, milk, chopped spinach, and seasoning in large bowl.
Beat until eggs are mixed well.

Add mixture to pre-browned shell and put back in oven for
approximately 1 hour.

Cool. Cut into quarters. Enjoy with fresh fruit.

Serves 4 to 6 people

Natalia del Basso Orsini

NATALIA'S

NATALIA DEL BASSO ORSINI wants her customers to find more than fine dining at Natalia's. "I want them to find peace," she said. "Just come here and put yourself into our hands. Business people come here when they're done with their day of work, and they say we're like an oasis."

Whether you're there for a couple of drinks in the bar, run by Natalia's husband, Daniel Underwood, or for a memorable meal, you'll find the experience delightful. Natalia's has been charming guests for 25 years. The charm originates in Natalia herself, whose voice is rich with the accents of her Italian homeland and whose manner is as warm as if she were greeting guests in her home.

The ambience of the dining room complements every aspect of fine dining: perfectly appointed tables and service, subtle lighting, rich colors, and classical music. Italian Pagliacci (clowns) and pottery from Natalia's collections are pure Italy. The paintings are by their son-in-law, artist Carl Phillips, and can be purchased.

The excellent menu includes some favorite foods from Natalia's childhood, such as the rabbit. "My favorite food is rabbit and, oh, it is so delicious with a sauce of my mother's recipe," Natalia said. "We buy from an organic farm, and we run it as a special."

Escargot is another of her favorites, bringing back pleasant childhood memories. Raised in Sulmona, a town older than Rome, Natalia often accompanied her father after a rainfall to collect snails. After the snails were cleaned in salt water and cooked, her mother would make the garlic-tomato sauce that Natalia replicates today, "and we would sit there with toothpicks and get the snails out of the shells and dip them in my mother's sauce."

When you want a meal to remember, Natalia's will not disappoint.

WILD MUSHROOM RISOTTO
WITH MAYTAG BLUE CHEESE

INGREDIENTS

1 1/2 ounces dried porcini mushrooms

1/2 cup olive oil

8 ounces assorted wild mushrooms, sliced

2 garlic cloves, minced

1 cup red wine

salt

fresh black pepper

48 ounces chicken broth

1 stick unsalted butter

1 medium onion, finely chopped

2 cups aborro rice

1/2 cup Maytag blue cheese, crumbled

3/4 cup freshly grated Parmigianino-Reggiano

parsley, chopped

PREPARATION

In a small bowl, cover the porcini mushrooms with 1 cup of hot water. Stir and let soak for 20-30 minutes. Squeeze the liquid from the mushrooms, reserving the liquid. Chop the porcinis and set aside. Strain the liquid through a fine sieve and set aside.

Heat olive oil in a sauté pan over medium heat. Once hot, add fresh mushrooms. Sauté, stirring often for 2-3 minutes. Add garlic and chopped porcini and cook for an additional 2 minutes. Add a 1/2 cup of red wine and simmer until almost all the wine is reduced. Season with salt and pepper and set aside. In a large saucepan, bring the chicken broth to a boil. Reduce heat and keep warm. Heat 1/2 of the stick of butter in a large saucepan over medium heat. When hot, add onion and cook until transparent, not brown. Add rice to the onion and stir for 2 minutes. Add the remaining 1/2 cup of red wine and cook until completely absorbed for about 2-4 minutes. Add a 1/2 cup of chicken broth. Add the mushroom mixture and the porcini liquid to the rice and stir. Once the liquid is absorbed, continue adding chicken broth, stirring frequently. Check the rice for doneness after 15-18 minutes. It should be served al dente. Once the rice is done, stir in the remaining 1/2 stick of butter and the blue cheese crumbles. Adjust the seasonings and stir in the Parmigianino and parsley. Serve immediately.

Serves 4

BAKED FISH IN PUFF PASTRY
WITH CRAB DUXELLE

INGREDIENTS

1 small onion, chopped

3 tablespoons butter

1/2 teaspoon dried thyme

4 ounces sliced mushrooms

salt and pepper to taste

2 pieces puff pastry 10-inches-by-15-inches, cut in half to equal 4, 5-inch-by-7 1/2-inch pieces

2 eggs, beaten

4, 6-ounce pieces of any white fish (grouper, halibut, snapper)

chopped parsley

4 ounces of your choice of crabmeat (king, lump, or claw)

PREPARATION

Preheat oven to 350 degrees.

DUXELLE Sauté onion in butter until transparent. Add thyme and mushrooms and cook on low heat until mushrooms are tender. Season with salt and pepper. Cool mixture.

PASTRY Place puff pastry on floured surface, long-ways, facing you. Brush ends with egg wash. Place fish on bottom half of pastry and season with salt and pepper.

Divide cooled duxelle mixture into 4 portions and place a 1/4 of mixture on top of each fish. Sprinkle with parsley and top with desired crabmeat.

Fold top of puff pastry down over fish and press edges together sealing well. Brush with egg wash and bake in 350-degree oven until pastry is golden and fish is cooked through, about 20 minutes.

Serves 2

CHOCOLATE HAZELNUT TORTE

PREPARATION

Preheat oven to 375 degrees.

Lightly butter and flour a 9-inch round spring form pan.

To make the torte, spread the 1/2 cup of hazelnuts on a baking sheet and toast in the oven until lightly brown and fragrant, 5-7 minutes. While the nuts are still warm, place them in a kitchen towel and rub with the towel to remove the skins. Do not worry if bits of skin remain. Set aside.

Place the chocolate and butter in a large metal mixing bowl set over gently simmering water in a pan. Stir often until the chocolate melts, then remove from the heat.

In a food processor fitted with the metal blade, combine the skinned nuts with a 1/2 cup of sugar. Pulse until finely ground. Add to the chocolate mixture and stir until well blended. Let cool, and then add the egg yolks, beating well after each addition. In a bowl, sift together the flour and cocoa. Stir into the chocolate mixture.

In another bowl, using an electric mixer beat the egg whites and cream of tartar until soft peaks form. Add 2 tablespoons of sugar and beat until stiff peaks form. Using a spatula, stir in a 1/4 of the whites into the chocolate mixture to lighten it. Fold in the remaining whites just until no white streaks remain. Pour into the prepared pan.

Bake until skewer inserted into the center comes out almost clean, 35-40 minutes. Let cool in the pan on a rack.

To make the glaze, combine the chocolate, butter, and corn syrup in a metal mixing bowl set over gently simmering water in a pan. Stir often until smooth. Let cool, stirring occasionally, for 15 minutes; it will thicken slightly.

Invert the torte onto a rack set over a baking sheet and lift off the pan. Pour on the glaze, tilting the torte to coat the top and sides completely. When the glaze stops dripping, place the 12 hazelnuts around the top. Transfer to serving plate.

INGREDIENTS

TORTE

¹/₂ cup hazelnuts, plus 12 hazelnuts for garnish

6 ounces bittersweet chocolate, finely chopped

¹/₂ cup plus 2 tablespoons sugar

5 eggs, separated

¹/₄ cup all-purpose flour

¹/₄ cup unsweetened cocoa

¹/₈ teaspoon cream of tartar

2 sticks of butter

GLAZE

9 ounces bittersweet chocolate, chopped

³/₄ cup unsalted butter, at room temperature, cut into small pieces

¹/₄ cup corn syrup

Makes one 9-inch torte; serves 10

THE RED TOMATO

"IF YOU'RE DINING at The Red Tomato you're special," says the restaurant's chef, Michael Falduti, Jr. "Everybody's special," Falduti said. "If you're sitting in my seats, you're family to me."

The pristine white and red color scheme is just the beginning at The Red Tomato, located on North Alexander Street in Bolingbroke. Whether you dine indoors or under the lazily-turning ceiling fans on the delightful veranda, the experience is memorable for both food and service.

Red Tomato's menu includes "all kinds of classical French cuisine to Southern barbecue pig pickin'," said Falduti, whose family members—wife, son, mom, dad, sister and others—all have roles to play at the restaurant.

Falduti, who grew up in Macon, got his introduction to kitchen skills from his mom, who by all reports is an excellent cook. His formal training began at the former Leo's restaurant in Macon, after which he went on to work in Charleston, South Carolina, at Maxim's in Paris, Emeril's in New Orleans and the Fish House in Las Vegas—as well as working with Las Vegas top chef, Andre Rochat, where he got his fine dining roots before coming home and opening The Red Tomato in 2004.

Falduti has translated his blend of Italian family background and Southern upbringing into a menu that offers an eclectic mix of Southern and Continental dining. Favorite dishes among his customers range from pan-seared Ahi tuna, to blackeyed pea cakes. Repeat customers also frequently order the rack of lamb, Pineapple Soup, ostrich or pork osso bucco.

The Red Tomato draws customers from out of state as well as from all points in Georgia, including Atlanta. The restaurant was winner of the 2008 and 2009 Foodie Award for Best Neighborhood Restaurant presented by *M Food & Culture* magazine.

Michael Falduti, Jr.

TUNA TARTAR
WITH WASABI BASIL OIL

INGREDIENTS

WASABI BASIL OIL

1 bunch basil leaves, steamed

1/4 teaspoon wasabi paste

1 cup oil (olive or vegetable)

1/2 teaspoon sea salt,
freshly ground

TUNA TARTAR

12 ounces tuna filet, finely diced

2 teaspoons extra virgin olive oil

4-6 large basil leaves, minced

zest of one lemon, finely chopped

1/2 teaspoon sea salt,
freshly ground

ground black pepper to taste

GARNISH

4 quail eggs

pickled ginger

Wasabi Basil Oil

PREPARATION

WASABI BASIL OIL In a food processor, combine the basil, wasabi paste, oil, and sea salt and puree until smooth. Pour through a fine strainer and set the oil aside in the refrigerator.

TUNA TARTAR In a medium bowl, combine all of the ingredients, tossing gently to coat and incorporate. Set aside.

TO SERVE Fill a small 3-ounce, dome-shaped mold with some tartar, pressing gently. Unmold onto the center of the plate and press lightly to make an indentation. Garnish with quail egg, pickled ginger and a drizzle of Wasabi Basil Oil.

Serves 4

GRILLED LAMB CHOPS
WITH CARAMELIZED SHALLOT SAUCE

INGREDIENTS

LAMB CHOPS

2 tablespoons olive oil

3, 4-ounce lamb chops per person

salt and pepper to taste

SHALLOT SAUCE

1 tablespoon olive oil

8 large shallots, peeled

4 cups red wine

2 cups lamb stock

salt and pepper to taste

1 1/2 tablespoons unsalted butter

GARNISH

mint, cut into thin strips

shallot

PREPARATION

SHALLOT SAUCE In a medium deep sauté pan, heat oil over medium heat. Add shallots and sauté until light brown. Add the red wine and stock. Bring to a boil, reduce the heat, and simmer until shallots are very tender. Use a slotted spoon to remove shallots and simmer until the liquid is reduced to a thick consistency. Add the butter and stir to incorporate. Season and keep warm.

LAMB Preheat the oven to 325 degrees. In a large sauté pan, heat oil over medium heat. Season the lamb and sear on both sides. Transfer to a sheet pan, place in oven and cook to desired doneness. Keep warm.

TO SERVE Spoon some shallot red wine sauce around the dish and place the lamb chops in the center and sprinkle mint around the dish.

Serves 4

SAGE BACON WRAPPED SCALLOPS
WITH A ROASTED RED PEPPER COULIS

INGREDIENTS

SCALLOPS

12 slices bacon, partially cooked

12, 2-ounce scallops

1/4 bunch sage, stemmed and minced

salt and pepper to taste

1 tablespoon pork fat

COULIS

2 cups heavy cream

1 pound red peppers, fire-roasted and seeded

salt and pepper to taste

GARNISH

diced tomato

bacon strips

fried sage leaves

PREPARATION

SCALLOPS Lay the slices of bacon on a flat working surface. Sprinkle each scallop with sage and season. Wrap with a slice of bacon and set aside. In a large sauté pan, melt the pork fat over medium heat. Add the scallop bacon side down and sauté to desired doneness. Remove from heat and keep warm.

ROASTED RED PEPPER COULIS In a medium saucepan, bring the cream to a boil and remove from heat. Add the sage and set aside to infuse until slightly cool. Transfer to a food processor and puree until smooth. Strain through a fine sieve and transfer to a saucepan over medium heat. Simmer until warm throughout. Remove from heat and season. Keep warm.

TO SERVE Spoon some Red Pepper Coulis onto center of plate and arrange scallops and three mounds of diced tomatoes.

Garnish with crispy bacon and fried sage.

Serves 4

GOLDEN PINEAPPLE AND VANILLA SOUP
WITH RUM ICE CREAM

INGREDIENTS

ICE CREAM

1 cup milk

1 cup heavy cream

1/2 cup granulated sugar

1 vanilla bean, split

5 egg yolks

1/4 cup dark rum

SOUP

1 small pineapple, steamed, peeled, cored, coarsely chopped, and pureed

2 cups golden pineapple juice

1 vanilla bean, split

1 1/2 tablespoons honey

3 ounces Muscat de Beaumes de Venise

juice of 2 limes

GARNISH

pineapple leaves

diced pineapple

PREPARATION

ICE CREAM In a medium saucepan, combine the milk, cream, half of the sugar and the vanilla bean, and bring to a boil. Remove from the heat and set aside to infuse for 15 minutes. In a small bowl, whisk together the remaining sugar and egg yolks. Remove the cream from the heat and temper the egg yolks, adding a third of the boiled cream while whisking constantly. Add the rum, whisk the tempered egg back into the cream, and place over medium heat, stirring constantly with a wooden spoon. When the mixture thickens enough to coat the back of the spoon, remove from the heat and pour through a fine strainer. Cool in an ice bath and freeze in an ice cream machine according to machine directions.

SOUP In a medium saucepan, combine the pineapple puree, juice, vanilla bean, and honey and bring to a boil. Remove from heat, cover, and set aside to infuse for 20 minutes. Remove the vanilla bean. Pour into a blender or a food processor and puree until smooth. Add the wine and lime juice and set aside in the refrigerator to chill.

SERVE Ladle some soup into a chilled bowl, place ice cream in the center, and garnish with pineapple leaves and diced pineapple.

Serves 4

80

Dargan McAfee, Jr.

THE SHAMROCK

GREAT FOOD and a full bar are just the beginning at The Shamrock in Payne City. Repeat customers have been enjoying the restaurant's pub atmosphere and good food for years. "A lot of people think The Shamrock is just a bar, and we do serve alcohol and we do have live music," said owner and host Dargan McAfee, Jr., "but we serve all kinds of good food. A lot of families enjoy coming here. We get families, college students, retired people, just a mixed array."

Dargan has been managing The Shamrock since it opened in 1995, and his wife, Liz, well known for her creative recipes, is the cook. If pub food is your choice, The Shamrock offers wings, burgers, shepherd's pie, corned beef and the like. And Liz creates an ever-changing menu of delicious fine-dining dishes such as shrimp with clam sauce and bourbon-marinated salmon.

There's a great ribeye, too, and popular fried shrimp or fried oyster po' boys. Liz also specializes in salads that are a full meal and presents seasonal dishes including casseroles for chilly evenings. "Liz is always coming up with new recipes," said Dargan. "She reads cookbooks and watches the (cooking) shows and enjoys creating new dishes."

Families are welcome at The Shamrock anytime, and they especially like to show up for lunch on Sundays. In pleasant weather, you can dine on the delightful patio in the shade of a mulberry tree.

On Tuesdays, live music begins about 7:30; on weekends it's later, about 9:30 or 10. Thursday night is Trivia Night. "It's a tradition, it's fun, and you learn something, too," Dargan said.

They're closed Mondays, but every other night brings good food and good times at The Shamrock.

SALMON CROQUETTES
SERVED WITH LEMON MUSTARD SAUCE

INGREDIENTS

CROQUETTES

1 1/2 pounds fresh baked salmon filets (bake with olive oil, salt & pepper)

1–1 1/2 cups chopped fresh bread crumbs

1 beaten egg

1/3 cup chopped onion

1/3 cup chopped celery

1/2 tablespoon yellow mustard

1 tablespoon mayo

salt and white pepper to taste

Good Dash Old Bay

pinch of parsley

LEMON MUSTARD SAUCE

1/4 cup mayonnaise

1/4 cup sour cream

2 large lemons (juice and zest)

2 tablespoons yellow mustard

2 tablespoons white vinegar

pinch salt and pinch white pepper

PREPARATION

Preheat oven to 350 degrees.

CROQUETTES Brush salmon filets with olive oil, salt and pepper to taste. Bake for 10 minutes or until done. Remove from oven and cool.

In mixing bowl, mix filets with the other ingredients. Chill mixture in refrigerator.

Pat out into 4 to 6 croquettes. Pan sauté in butter until golden brown.

Top each croquette with Lemon Mustard Sauce.

MUSTARD SAUCE Combine all the ingredients and mix well.

Serves 4 to 6

SPINACH CASSEROLE

INGREDIENTS

1-pound carton cottage cheese

1/4 cup butter

2 cups sharp cheddar cheese

4 beaten eggs

4 tablespoons flour

2 packaged chopped frozen spinach cooked and drained (2, 10-ounce boxes)

2 cloves chopped garlic

1 medium chopped onion

salt and white pepper, to taste

nutmeg and red pepper ground, to taste

PREPARATION

In a 9-inch sauté pan, melt a 1/4 cup butter, sauté onions and garlic over medum heat. Let cool. Add cheese, beaten eggs, flour and cottage cheese. Add spinach, salt, pepper, nutmeg and cayenne pepper.

Place in greased casserole dish, add bread crumbs and cook at 350 degrees for 45 minutes to 1 hour.

Serves 4 to 6

GREEK STYLE GRILLED CHICKEN

INGREDIENTS

MARINADE

1/3 cup red wine vinegar

salt and pepper

dash paprika

1/2 teaspoon herb seasoning

1/2 cup vegetable oil

TOPPING

3 medium tomatoes, diced

1 large Vidalia onion, diced

2 cloves garlic, minced

4 tablespoons olive oil

1 tablespoon lemon juice (fresh)

2 tablespoon Gourmet Garden
Italian seasoning herb blend

1 large seeded cucumber, diced

5 ounces kalamata olives

salt and white pepper

2 tablespoons red wine vinegar

dash Dijon mustard

PREPARATION

Marinate 4 to 6 boneless chicken breasts for 2 to 4 hours.

Mix the topping ingredients well, then refrigerate.

Grill chicken, cover with topping and sprinkle with crumbled
feta cheese.

Julio Rosas

TIC TOC ROOM

ATLANTA RESTAURATEUR Cesare Mammarella found the new location he wanted when he visited downtown Macon in 2000. "There's a charm about downtown—the buildings, the architecture, the alleyways—but I saw a need for something newer, edgier, than what was here," Cesare said. "I saw this building and I wanted it. The bare old brick walls, high ceilings and wood floors suggested a look that's both retro and modern."

The Tic Toc Room is a multiple award-winner and a favorite upscale spot for enjoying a drink or a bottle of fine wine with a memorable evening meal. And the dress-casual atmosphere provides a relaxing finale to any day. Cesare encourages his chef to invent new, enticing dishes. "I don't want to do what everybody else is doing; that's no fun," he said. "I challenge my chef to do different things, to think outside the box."

Chef Julio Rosas sets a high standard in the kitchen. Tic Toc's crab and lobster dip served with plantain chips has been a favorite from opening day. Customers love the unique Tuna Futomaki, and the lobster bisque is "to die for." The menu pulls from Asian, Caribbean, European and Latin cuisines, often teaming them with staples such as a filet or ribeye, salmon or crab cakes. "Chef Rosas is creative and fearless, and he knows how to apply different ingredients," Cesare said, and then he grinned, "And there's also the famous sauce I'm not allowed to discuss."

Tic Toc's award-winning piano bar complements the restaurant. Known for its martinis and their old-school presentation with sidecar, the bar stocks thirty-five vodkas and other pleasant potables making it a fun place to sit, sip, and meet and greet friends.

It's all just off the Cherry Street Plaza on Martin Luther King Jr. Boulevard.

CHILI RUBBED TIGER SHRIMP
WITH ORANGE-LIME GLAZE

INGREDIENTS

24 black tiger shrimp
deveined, tails on

*(If tiger shrimp are unavailable,
any large shrimp will suffice.)*

1/2 cup vegetable oil

RUB

4 tablespoons chili powder

2 teaspoons garlic powder

1 teaspoon salt

2 teaspoons paprika

3 teaspoons cumin

GLAZE

1/2 cup orange marmalade

grated peel and juice of 2 limes

4 tablespoons honey

PREPARATION

Combine rub ingredients and pat onto shrimp.

Heat vegetable oil in a skillet over medium heat. Add shrimp and cook 1 minute on each side.

Mix glaze ingredients and keep warm until ready to serve.

Garnish with lemon wedge.

Serves 6

TIC TOC ROOM OSSO BUCCO

INGREDIENTS

4 veal shanks
flour for dusting
2 onions, diced
1 cup celery, diced
2 bay leaves

salt for seasoning
1 cup olive oil
1 large carrot, diced
3 tablespoons tomato, diced
red wine

PREPARATION

Preheat oven to 300 degrees.

Season the veal with the salt and dust with the flour in a heat proof casserole dish. Sauté the veal with the olive oil until both sides are golden brown. Set aside.

In the same pan, sauté onions, carrots, and celery for 3 minutes. Add tomatoes, bay leaves, and red wine. Return the veal to the pan and add water just to cover the shanks.

Cover and bake at 300 degrees for 3 hours or until veal is tender.

Remove the veal from the sauce and keep warm.

Reduce and puree the sauce. Add salt and pepper. Pour the sauce over the veal shanks and serve with polenta or risotto and asparagus.

Serves 4

BLUE FIN CAJUN TUNA
WITH MANGO CHUTNEY

INGREDIENTS

MANGO CHUTNEY

1 mango, diced

1 tablespoon red pepper, diced

1/2 cup raisins

1/2 cup brown sugar

1 cup water

1 tablespoon parsley

1 tablespoon corn starch

3 tablespoons water

TUNA

1/4 cup olive oil

1, 4-ounce steak of blue fin tuna, sushi quality

Cajun seasoning

salt and pepper, to season

Mango Chutney

sesame seeds, white and black

chili oil

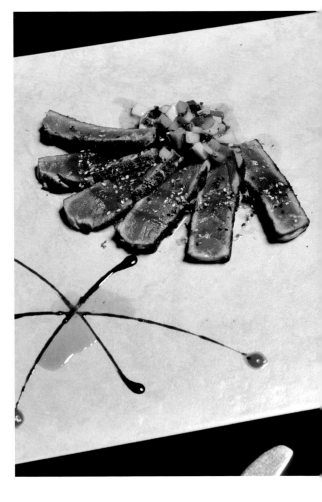

PREPARATION

CHUTNEY Mix mango, pepper, raisins, brown sugar, water, and parsley in a pan and bring to a boil.

In a separate bowl, mix corn starch and 3 tablespoons water together. Add corn starch mixture and salt and pepper to the chutney mix.

TUNA Preheat a heavy iron skillet with the olive oil. Pat tuna with Cajun seasoning. Sear tuna for 30 seconds on each side.

Slice tuna into thin slices and spoon chutney on top. Garnish with sesame seeds, parsley, and chili oil.

Serves 1

SKILLET SEARED
CHILEAN SALMON
WITH ORANGE MARMALADE AU JUS

INGREDIENTS

8 ounce steak salmon

olive oil

ORANGE MARMALADE AU JUS

1 cup orange marmalade

1/2 tablespoon corn starch

2 1/2 tablespoons soy sauce

2 1/2 tablespoons dry sherry

2 tablespoons brown sugar

1/2 cup chicken stock

2 teaspoons sesame oil

1 garlic clove minced

salt and pepper to season

PREPARATION

Preheat oven to 300 degrees.

Heat olive oil in skillet to medium heat. Sear seasoned salmon on both sides until golden brown, then bake salmon in the oven for 5 minutes.

Mix the rest of the ingredients.

Remove salmon from oven and add 1/2 of the sauce to the salmon to deglaze pan. Plate the salmon and heat the remaining juices in the same pan and pour over salmon.

Garnish with an orange slice.

Serves 1

Mike and Twila Faye Dunlap

TWILA FAYE'S TEA ROOM & SODA FOUNTAIN

REMEMBER SODA FOUNTAINS? You don't see them much anymore, but there's one at Twila Faye's Tea Room and Soda Fountain on Highway 41 in Bolingbroke.

At Twila Faye's, you can have a great lunch or weekend supper and top it off with premium hand-dipped ice cream. The friendly folks at Twila Faye's will bring you a single scoop or more, all the way up to a banana split. Mike and Twila Faye Dunlap have owned Twila Faye's since 2002, and it attracts regional customers as well as tourists from out of state.

When the Dunlaps purchased the restaurant it was a tea room called Sweet Sue's, and Twila Faye was a waitress there, a waitress with a dream. She wanted to own an authentic Southern-style restaurant, using her own recipes for dishes like black-eyed peas, country-fried steak, pan-fried salmon patties, and collard greens. So, she and Mike decided to keep the tea room and add Southern cooking. Twila is the cook, and some of her cake recipes are her mother's.

Her repeat customers say the only difficult thing about dining at Twila Faye's is deciding what to eat. The menu is packed with soups, salads, sandwiches, quiches and casseroles. Her chicken salad is especially popular and so is the Praline Pie. And the homemade brownies are especially tasty if you order that hand-dipped ice cream to go with them. No one leaves Twila Faye's hungry.

Twila Faye also creates party trays and caters events such as luncheons, baby or wedding showers, and Red Hat Society gatherings. The restaurant has a private banquet room set aside for these festivities.

"You can call to reserve a date for your special occasion," Twila Faye said. "Let us do all the work and clean up for you."

PRALINE PIE

INGREDIENTS

STEP ONE

1/2 cup oatmeal

1/2 cup pecan halves

2 teaspoons whole wheat flour

FILLING

1 stick melted butter or margarine

1/2 cup dark brown sugar

1/2 cup light brown sugar

1/2 cup granulated sugar

2 eggs, beaten

1/8 teaspoon baking powder

dash salt

1 teaspoon vanilla

PREPARATION

STEP ONE In pie pan, bake until oats and pecans are toasted. Approximately 10-15 minutes at 350 degrees. Set aside and prepare filling.

STEP TWO In a medium bowl, mix butter and sugars well.

Add eggs, baking powder, salt, and vanilla. Pour oat mixture into a 10-inch, deep-dish pie shell.

Cover with filling and bake at 350 degrees for 30-35 minutes or until barely set.

Serves 8

TEA BREAD PUFFS

INGREDIENTS

1 cup water

1 stick butter

1/2 teaspoon salt

1 cup all-purpose flour

4 eggs

PREPARATION

Preheat oven to 400 degrees.

In a medium sauce pan combine water and butter. Bring to a boil until butter is thoroughly melted. In a medium bowl, sift together salt and flour. Add to liquid at low heat and stir until mixed well. (It should resemble mashed potatoes in texture.)

Transfer above ingredients to mixer. Add 4 eggs, one at a time, and mix well (1-2 minutes) for each egg, thus ensuring air into puff mix. When dough is ready it should have a "glossy" look.

Put into pastry bag and squeeze in a circular motion quarter-size puffs onto a sheet pan lined with parchment paper. Bake at 400 degrees for 20-25 minutes. Complete by stuffing with chicken or tuna salad.

A tasty appetizer and eye-pleasing party tray. Great at bridal or baby showers, church socials, or small parties.

Serves 8 (approx. 6 each)

SOUTHERN VIDALIA ONION QUICHE

INGREDIENTS

1 stick butter

4 sliced onions

3 tablespoons plain flour

1/4 teaspoon salt

1/4 teaspoon pepper

1, 10-inch unbaked pie shell

2 cups swiss cheese, grated

3 eggs

1 1/2 cups milk

4 tomatoes, thinly sliced

breadcrumbs (optional)

PREPARATION

Melt butter in sauce pan. Add onions, flour, salt, and pepper and sauté until soft, approximately 5 minutes. Drain juice.

In unbaked pie shell add 1 cup of swiss cheese and pour in sautéed ingredients. Add remaining cup of swiss cheese.

In a small bowl beat 3 eggs until frothy. Add 1 1/2 cups milk and mix well.

Pour egg-milk mixture into pie shell. Top with thinly sliced tomatoes. Add breadcrumbs if desired. Bake at 350 degrees for 25-30 minutes.

Savor this sweet onion pie with a garden salad and fresh fruit. Excellent as a brunch delight or served as a main course.

Serves 8

CHOCOLATE SODA

INGREDIENTS

1 ounce chocolate syrup
1 ounce whole milk
carbonated water
vanilla ice cream
whipping cream
1 whole maraschino cherry

PREPARATION

Add chocolate syrup and milk, stir thoroughly, add a small amount of carbonated water, one scoop of vanilla ice cream, and top with additional carbonated water. Add whipping cream in a spiral motion and top with cherry.

Serves 1

BANANA NUT BREAD

INGREDIENTS

9 large bananas, ripe until dark
1½ cups vegetable oil
2 tablespoons vanilla
6 eggs, beaten
6 cups plain flour
3 cups sugar
1½ tablespoons baking soda
2½ cups finely chopped pecans or walnuts

PREPARATION

Freeze bananas overnight and thaw in order to obtain the best flavor of the available juice. Mash thoroughly.

In a large mixing bowl, mix bananas, vegetable oil, vanilla, and eggs. In separate bowl, mix dry ingredients; stir thoroughly. Mix dry ingredients slowly into banana mixture. Do not "over mix" as this causes bread to fall. Pour into 4 greased and floured bread pans.

Bake at 325 degrees for 35-45 minutes or until probe comes out clean.

Yield: 4 large loaves

RESTAURANT GUIDE

DOLCE VITA PIZZERIA & CAFE
484 Cherry Street
Macon, GA 31201
(478)257-6440
hotplatesrestaurantgroup.com

DOWNTOWN GRILL
562 Mulberry Street Lane
Macon, GA 31201
macondowntowngrill.com

GRITS CAFE
17 West Johnston Street
Forsyth, GA 31029
(478) 994-8325
gritscafe.com

JENEANE'S
4436 Forsyth Road
Macon, GA 31210
(478) 476-4642
jeneanes.com

KUDZU CATERING
3508 Brookdale Avenue
Macon, GA 31204
(478) 743-8200
kudzucatering.com

LUIGI'S BISTRO
401 Cherry Street
Macon, GA 31201
(478) 743-4645
hotplatesrestaurantgroup.com

**MARCO
RISTORANTE ITALIANO**
4581 Forsyth Road
Macon, GA 31210
(478) 405-5660
marcomacon.com

MOLLY'S
402 Cherry St
Macon, GA 31201
(478) 744-9898

NATALIA'S
201 North Macon Street
Macon, Georgia 31210
(478) 741-1380
natalias.net

THE RED TOMATO
7248 North Alexander Court
Bolingbroke, Georgia 31004
(478) 994-6336

SHAMROCK
342 Rose Avenue #C
Macon, Georgia 31204
(478) 750-1555

TIC TOC ROOM
408 Martin Luther King Jr. Blvd
Macon, GA 31201
(478) 744-0123
hotplatesrestaurantgroup.com

**TWILA FAYE'S TEA ROOM
& SODA FOUNTAIN**
6025 U.S. Highway 41 South
Macon, GA 31210
(478) 994-0031

INDEX

BEAU CABELL has been shooting photos since age twelve, when an aunt and uncle lent him an old Kodak camera. A native Midwesterner and graduate of the University of Missouri, he developed into a freelance photojournalist for the *Atlanta Journal-Constitution* and several wire services and later worked for the *Savannah Morning News* before joining *The Macon Telegraph* in 1984.

He has won many awards for his work, and during his years at *The Telegraph* has become particularly interested in food photography. What inspired him to produce the photos for this cookbook, he said, were the excellent chefs and restaurateurs he was able to work with. "They were outstanding people who were able to lend a sense of place and context about the food," Beau said, "In food, the tricks of the trade are usually closely-guarded secrets, but these people were really open and ready to share so much of their expertise."

While Beau works exclusively with today's sophisticated cameras and equipment, he still treasures that old Kodak camera, which his uncle later gave to him as a gift.

SKIPPY DAVIS is a freelance writer in Macon, retired after thirty years in journalism, during which she won more than twenty-five state and national writing awards. For almost twenty of her years in newspapers she worked as a reporter, editor and columnist with *The (Macon) Telegraph*. She also was Southeast regional reporter for *Women's Wear Daily* and a fashion writer for *The Florida-Times Union*. In retirement, she enjoys gardening, making bead jewelry, working with animal rescue, and spending time with her three grown children and their families, which include seven absolutely adorable grandchildren.

REBUILDING MACON

OUR STORY

LET'S GET COOKING
REBUILDING MACON

THE SAME GOODNESS of people that has created our beautiful *Let's Get Cooking* is the identical kindness that insures the success of Rebuilding Macon. For almost two decades, dedicated volunteers have built homes, lives, and communities by helping their neighbors.

Founded in 1992, Rebuilding Macon reaches out to touch the lives of low-income elderly and disabled homeowners. Rebuilding Macon fills a pressing need in our community. The rising cost of living and falling social service budgets have left some of our most vulnerable neighbors without the most basic of necessities, a warm, safe, and dry home. Rebuilding Macon focuses on the concerns of the elderly and disabled low-income homeowner. By identifying the needs associated with these concerns, we are equipped to face a problem with full understanding and to create real solutions for the low-income homeowners we serve.

In partnership with the community, Rebuilding Macon rehabilitates the houses of low-income homeowners—free of charge, particularly the elderly and disabled, so that they may live in warmth, safety and independence.

In 1992, led by founder Bruce Gerwig and a determined board of directors, 300 volunteers repaired 18 homes on Saturday, April 24. From 1992 through 1998, more than 400 homes were repaired by community volunteers that planned for months in order to reach their goal of completing the repairs by the last Saturday in April. Thanks to a generous grant from the Peyton Anderson Foundation, in 1999, Rebuilding Macon became a year-round program. Established in 2002, a Fall Rebuilding Day was added, thanks to the Jaques Foundation.

In 2003, we created the Youth Enrichment Program which focuses on cultivating and mentoring teens and young adults in our home repair program. The youth enrichment program builds bridges between ages, ethnicities, physical challenges, and lifestyles. Our objectives include engaging young people in service projects that are challenging, rewarding and educational; serving the unmet needs of the community and its residents; promoting among young people a greater understanding & appreciation for the diversity of their community; and promoting a lifetime ethic of service among young people. The program has grown from 270 teen volunteers repairing 30 homes in 2003, to over 1,500 teens completing 120 repairs in 2010.

Between 1998 and 2009, we operated with one team of dedicated volunteers that each Tuesday worked to meet the needs of our homeowners. Today, we have three teams working Tuesdays, Wednesday and Thursdays to make sure that our elderly and disabled homeowners live in warmth, safety and independence.

Churches, businesses, and civic organizations are steadfast in the support of Rebuilding Macon. In 2010, over 2,500 volunteers gave their time, skills, and money to make a difference in the lives of all of us. Helping those in need improves the lives of everyone in Macon and Middle Georgia. At the end of the day, our volunteers leave with skinned knees, sore backs, and most importantly, a great sense of accomplishment.

In an effort to maintain funding to continue assisting our homeowners, Rebuilding Macon published *Let's Get Cooking*. All proceeds from the sale of this cookbook will support the programs of Rebuilding Macon.

The money raised by *Let's Get Cooking* will help build wheelchair ramps, replace roofs, paint homes and so much more. Give *Let's Get Cooking* to your friends and family to help rebuild Macon. Many hearts will be touched—especially your own!